— LONELY PLANET'S —

BEAUTIFUL WORLD

lonely planet

Melbourne | London | Oakland

ORIGINS

— 6 —

NOURISH

— 28 —

UNTAMED

— 52 —

COMMUNITY

— 78 —

CELEBRATION

— 102 —

TRANSFORMATION

— 122 —

SPACE

— 148 —

HARMONY

— 172 —

MONUMENTAL

— 196 —

ETERNAL

— 220 —

IT'S A
BEAUTIFUL
WORLD

———

Have you been to Yosemite Valley? That's a place that can make you catch your breath: the scale of the rock faces, the delirious perfection of the valley floor's meadows. It makes your head swim, a recognition of beauty so powerful, you just … stop.

The world is full of places like that. But we don't see them every day and sometimes we need to be reminded that they are there. This book gathers together photography of some of the world's most extraordinary places to share the wonder they bring.

Being in a beautiful place is more than observing what's before your eyes. The experience of beauty is an emotional one, brought about through context; there's the people you're with, or the people you're not with; there's your mood, where you are in your life. All these factors come together to make the response to a place unique and personal, and different every time you visit.

When you look at a photograph of a beautiful place, that context disappears. We thought about that fact when we were making this book. We wanted to create a context that helped bring some of those connections to bear. The images here are arranged in chapters that reflect an aspect of life. As you turn the pages we hope that pondering the relationship between each image and the life stage with which it's been connected will add another dimension to your experience.

The images in this book will take you to places far and wide, the kinds of places that you might never visit but that you can perhaps put on that "If" list we all have tucked away. These places are surprising, remarkable, remote, familiar … dive in and marvel over the undeniable fact; it *is* a beautiful world.

~ ORIGINS ~

The Milky Way. **The Dolomites, Italy** ⌃ |

Sulphuric lakes at Dallol. **Danakil Desert, Ethiopia** › |

Stone pinnacles at Cavusin. **Cappadocia, Turkey** ⌃ |

Moai (statues). **Easter Island, Pacific Ocean** ^

Adjder oasis. **Sahara Desert, Algeria** ‹ |

Rice terraces at Yuangyuan. **Yunnan, China** ^

Boab trees. **Western Australia** ⌃ ⎮

Kilauea volcano. **Hawaii, USA**

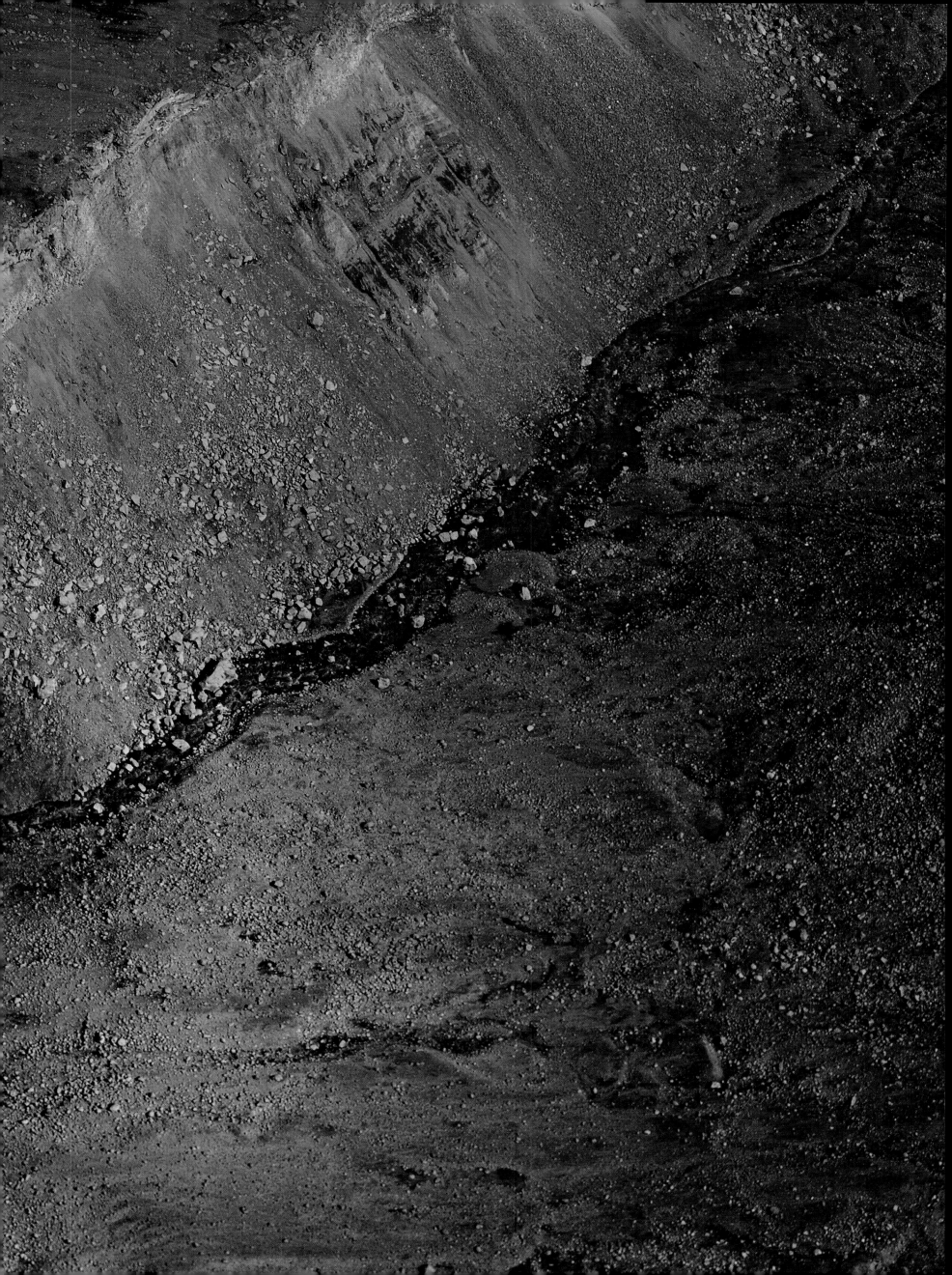

~ NOURISH ~

Okavango River. **Botswana** ︿ |

The Sardine Run. **Eastern Cape, South Africa** › |

Fruit trees at Pessines. **Charente-Maritime, France** ^

Elephant. **Masai Mara, Kenya**   ＾ |

Elephant herd. **Al-Sudd Swamp, South Sudan**   › |

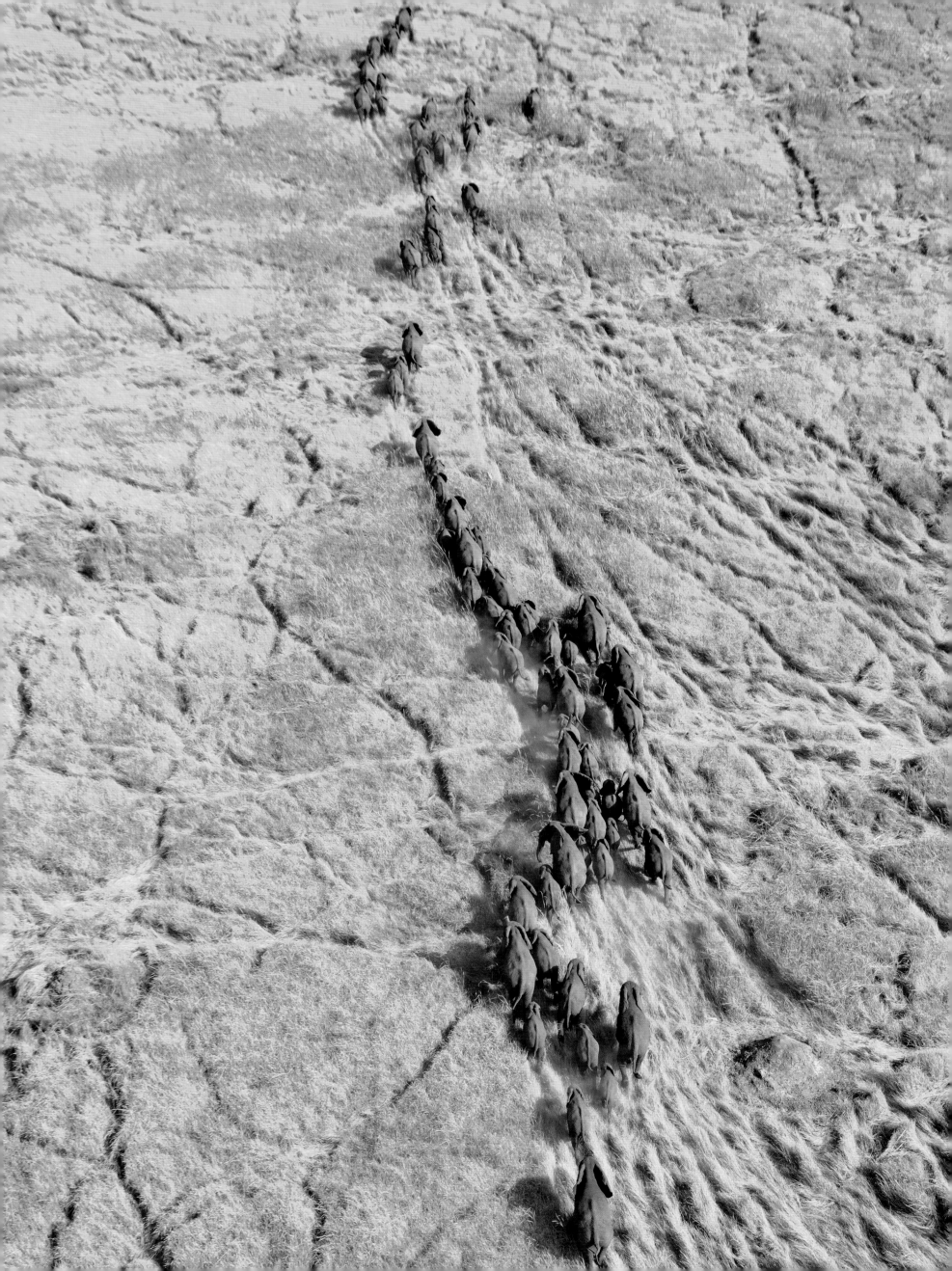

Steller's sea eagles. **Kamchatka, Russia** ⌃

Rice terraces. **Longsheng, China** ⌃ |

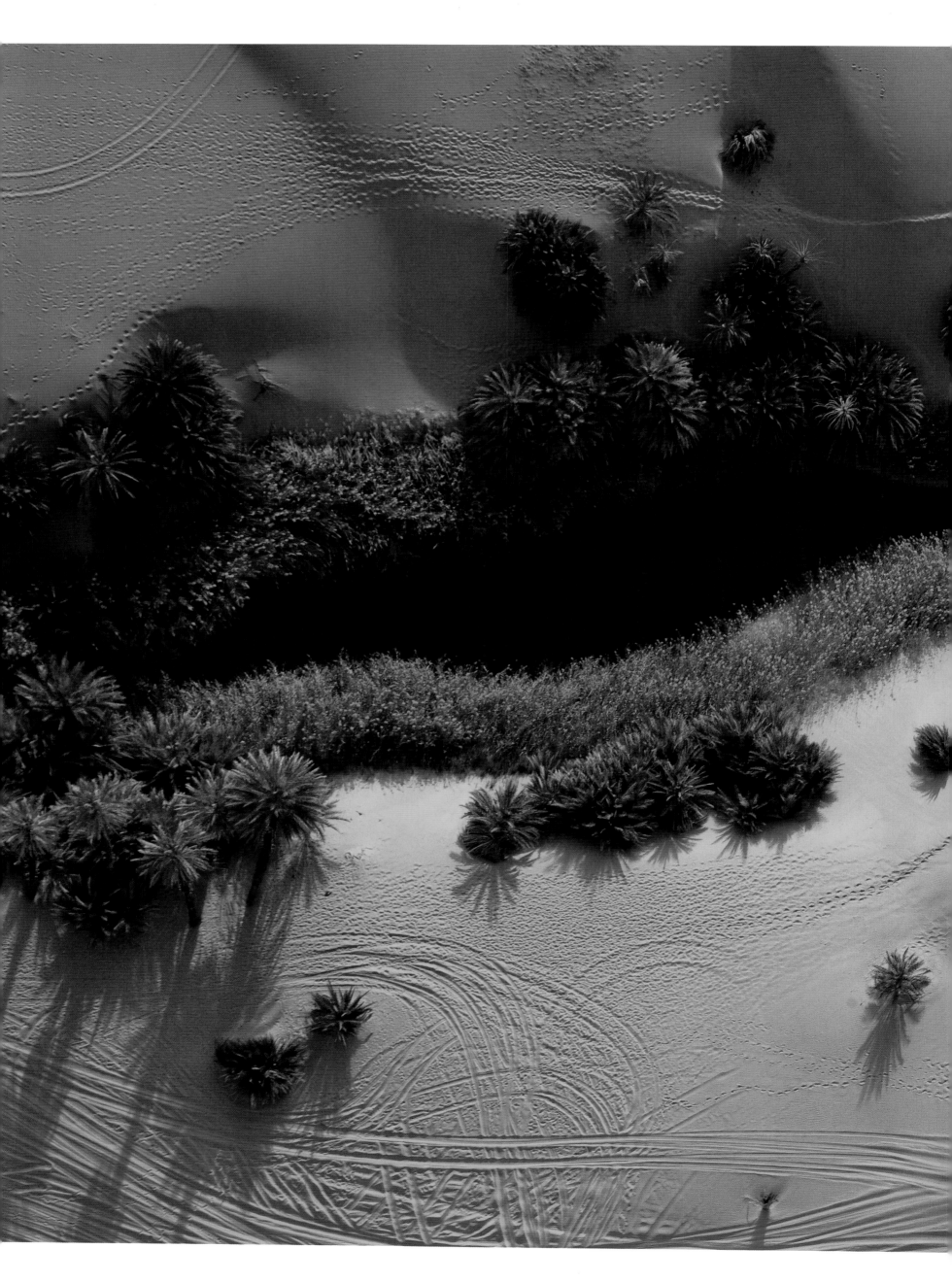

Incahuasi Island. **Salar de Uyuni, Bolivia** ‹ |

Li River. **Guangxi Zhuang, China** › |

Lavender on the Plateau de Valensole. **Alpes de Haute-Provence, France** ^ |

Lyth Valley in the Lake District. **Cumbria, England** ˄

Hippopotamus with egret. **Serengeti National Park, Tanzania** ⌃ |

UNTAMED

The Na Pali coast of Kaua'i. **Hawaii, USA** ^ | Surfing Phantoms at O'ahu. **Hawaii, USA** › |

Eyjafjallajökull volcano. **Iceland** ⌃ |

Nideck waterfall. **Alsace, France** ⌃ |

Ta Prohm temple. **Angkor Wat, Cambodia** ^ |

Lava from Kilauea volcano. **Hawaii, USA** ▴

Pinware River. **Labrador, Canada** ⌃

Torres del Paine National Park. **Patagonia, Chile** ^ |

Iguazú Falls. **Brazil–Argentina border** ˄

The Tarkine wilderness. **Tasmania, Australia** ^ |

Great White shark. **Gaudalupe Island, Mexico**

Avalanche. **Rhône-Alpes, France**

COMMUNITY

Beni Isguen. **Ghardaïa, Algeria** ⌃ |

The Great Barrier Reef. **Queensland, Australia** ＾ |

Water buffalo. **Ban Gioc, Vietnam** ^

Green turtles. **Galápagos Islands, Ecuador** ▴

Red deer in Richmond Park. **London, England** ⌃ |

Halong Bay. **Gulf of Tonkin, Vietnam** › |

Monarch Butterfly Biosphere Reserve. **Michoacán, Mexico**

Manarola town in Cinque Terre. **Liguria, Italy**

A water hole in Etosha National Park. **Namibia** ^ |

Vidigal favela. **Rio de Janeiro, Brazil** ^ |

Reine village. **Lofoten Islands, Norway** ^

CELEBRATION

Xoxo cemetery. **Oaxaca, Mexico** ‹

Black-browed albatross. **South Georgia Island, Atlantic Ocean** ᐱ |

The Sardine Run. **Eastern Cape, South Africa** ▲

Snow geese and sandhill cranes. **New Mexico, USA** ⌃ |

Polar bear. **Churchill, Canada** ^ |

Vineyards in Greve. **Tuscany, Italy** ⌃ |

Danum Valley Conservation Area. **Borneo, Malaysia** ‸ |

~ TRANSFORMATION ~

Monument Valley Tribal Park. **Arizona–Utah, USA** ^ |

TRANSFORMATION

Reed Flute Cave. **Guangxi, China** ^ |

Yellowstone National Park. **Wyoming, USA** › |

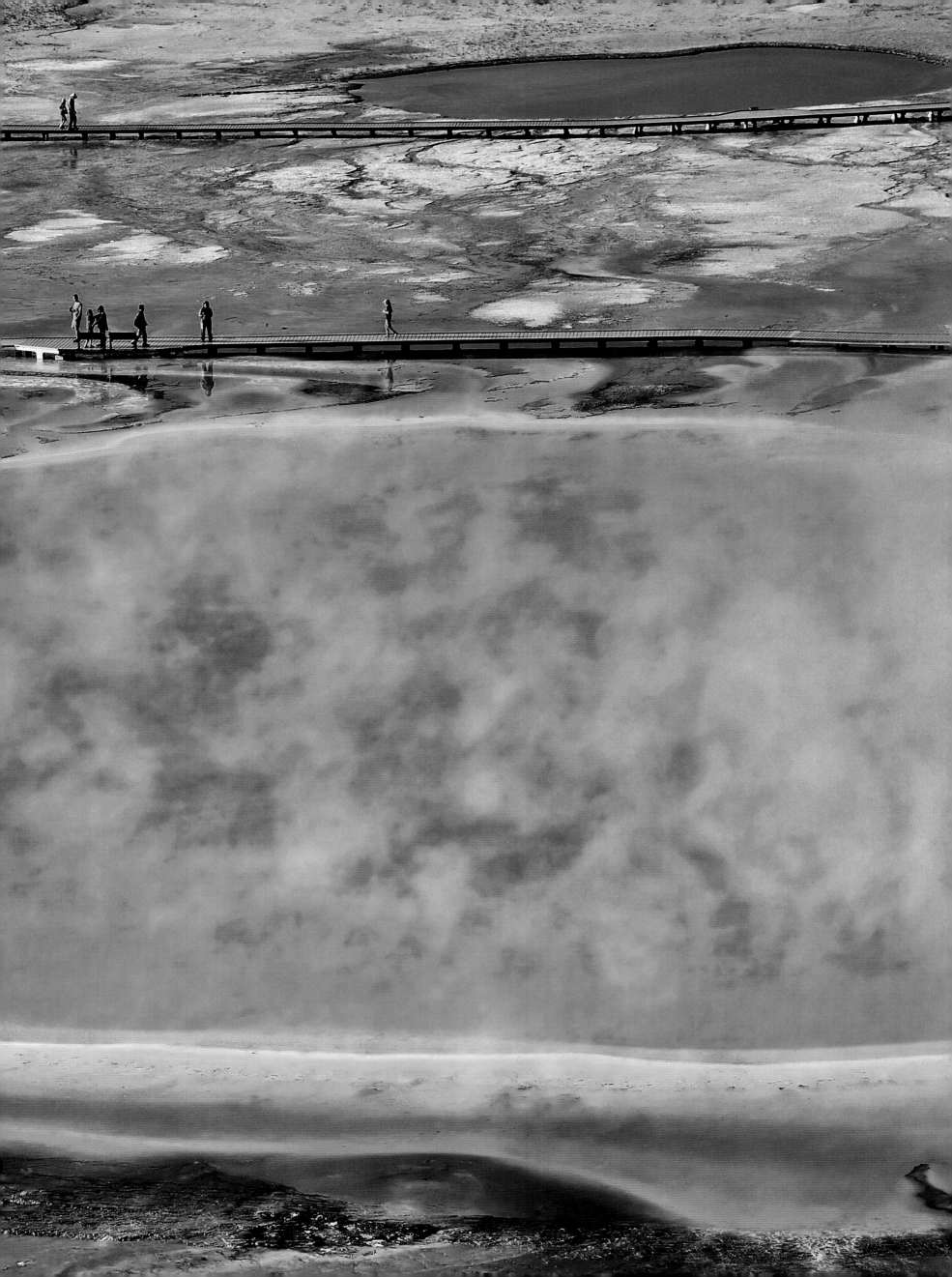

Wildflowers in the Mojave Desert. **California, USA** ˄

Drakes Passage. **The Southern Ocean, Antarctica** ^ |

Zhangye Danxia Landform Geological Park. **Gansu, China** ⌃ |

Nashua River. **New Hampshire, USA** › |

Bora Bora. **French Polynesia, Pacific Ocean** ⌃

A supercell storm near Alvo. **Nebraska, USA** ⌃

Gates of the Arctic National Park and Preserve. **Alaska, USA** ^ |

Iceberg in Grandidier Channel. **Pleneau Island, Antarctica** › |

Eyjafjallajökull volcano. **Iceland** ⌃

TRANSFORMATION

Grand Canyon. **Arizona, USA** ^ |

Skógafoss. **Iceland** ▸ |

- S P A C E -

Seljalandsfoss. **Iceland** ^ |

A cenote near Valladolid. **Yucatán, Mexico** ⌃ |

Mt Civetta. **The Dolomites, Italy** ▲

Hammerhead sharks. **Galápagos Islands, Ecuador** ›

Oneonta Creek, Columbia River Gorge. **Oregon, USA** ‹ |

~ HARMONY ~

Pura Ulun Danu Bratan temple. **Bali, Indonesia** ‹

The Devil's Marbles in Tennant Creek. **Northern Territory, Australia** ⌃ |

Red-crowned cranes. **Hokkaido, Japan** ⌃ | ›

Inuit hunter. **Qaanaaq, Greenland** ‹ |

Mustering horses. **Xilin Gol, Mongolia** ^ |

Moraine Lake in Banff National Park. **Alberta, Canada** ⌃

Highland cattle. **Scotland** ⌃ |

The Cuillins. **Isle of Skye, Scotland** ^ |

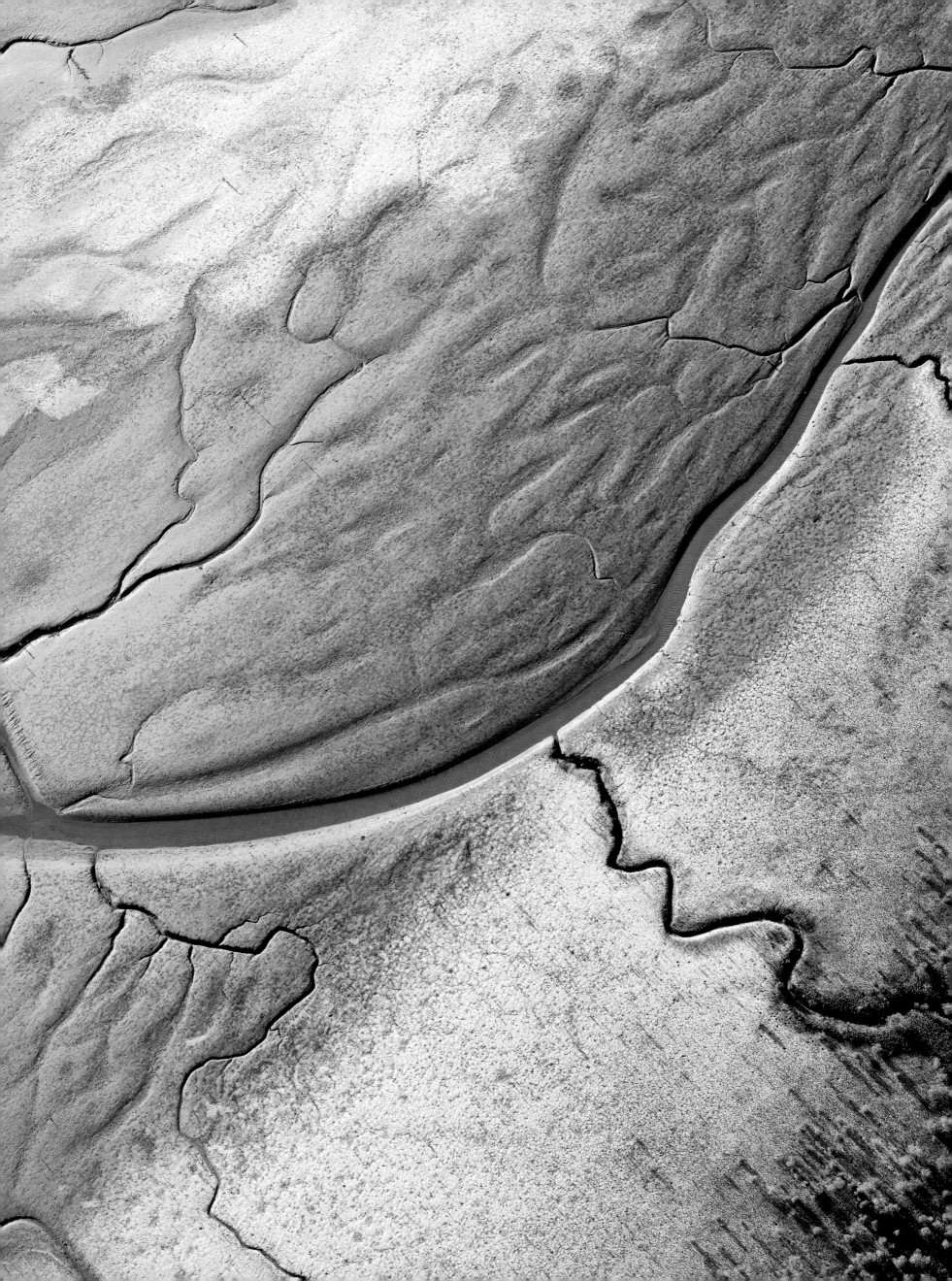

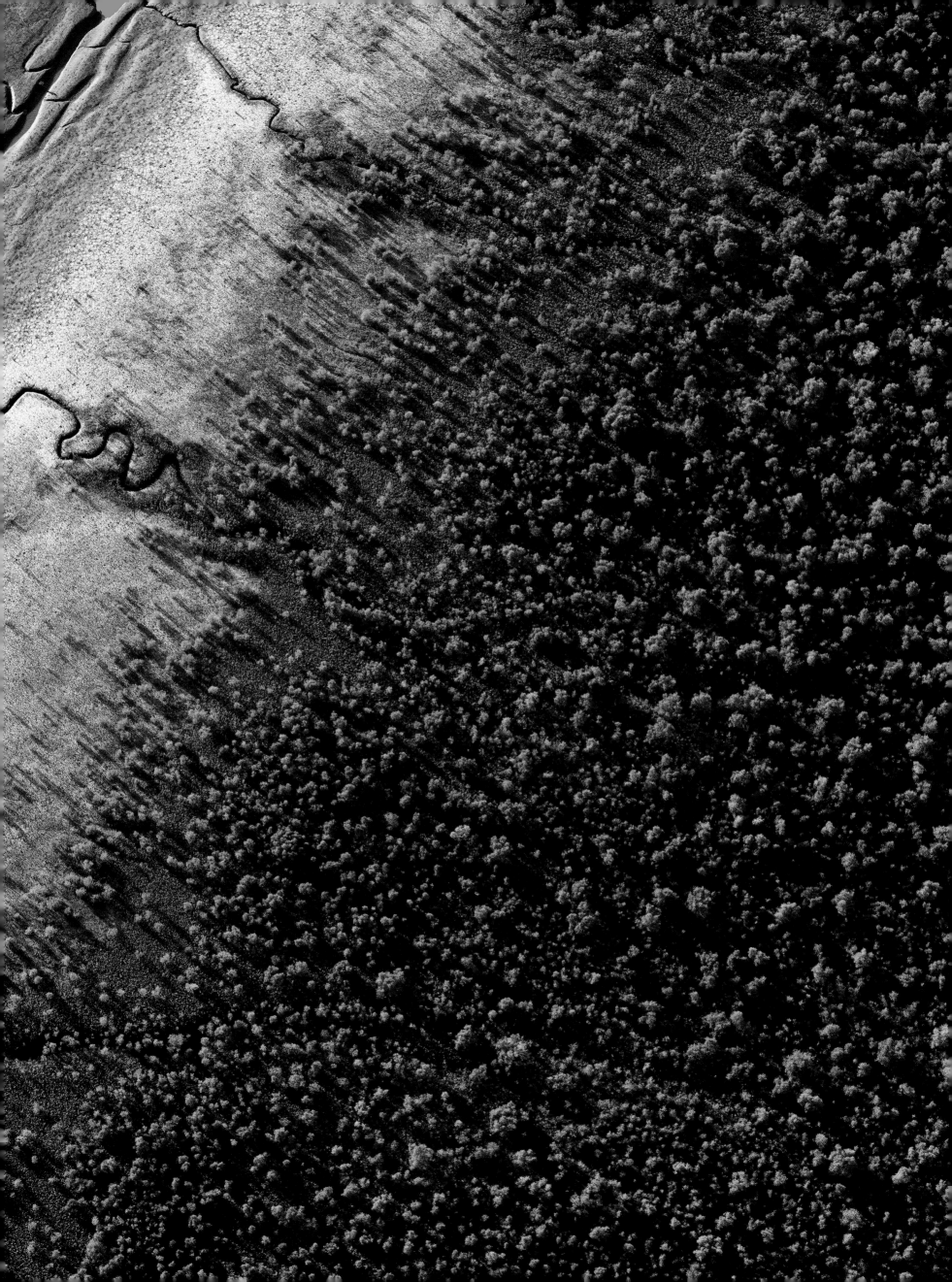

A quiver tree. **Kalahari, Namibia–South Africa** ^

The Kamakura Bamboo Garden. **Tokyo, Japan** ⌃

Lamayuru Monastery. **Ladakh, India** ⌃

Rice paddies. **Bali, Indonesia** ʌ |

Tianmen mountain road. **Hunan, China** ⌃ |

~ MONUMENTAL ~

Victoria Falls. **Zambia–Zimbabwe** ˄ |

Bryce Canyon National Park. **Utah, USA** ˄ |

The Gasherbrum massif. **Karakorum, Pakistan** ^ |

Nabiyotum volcano. **Lake Turkana, Kenya** ▲ |

Whale shark. **Western Australia** ▲

Ningaloo National Park. **Western Australia** ‹ |

Monument Valley. **Arizona–Utah, USA** › |

‹ The Palace of Westminster. **London, England**

Giraffes. **Okavango Delta, Botswana** ˄

The Kogelberg coast. **Western Cape, South Africa** ∧ |

~ ETERNAL ~

The Royal Tomb. **Petra, Jordan** ⌃

Pipeline, O'ahu. **Hawaii, USA** ‸ |

The Wave, Coyote Buttes. **Arizona–Utah, USA** ᴧ |

Taj Mahal. **Uttar Pradesh, India** ▴

Zabriskie Point, Death Valley. **California, USA** ^ |

Terracotta army, Xi'an. **Shaanxi, China** ^ | ›

The Temple of Saturn. **Rome, Italy** ▲

Bristlecone pine tree. **California, USA** ^ |

Saint-Trojan-les-Bains. **Île d'Oléron, France** ▲

Chamonix. **Rhône-Alpes, France** ‹

~ INDEX ~

Sequoia National Park.
California, USA

The General Sherman Tree, a sequoia found in California's Sequoia National Park, is the world's largest tree. It is more than 83m tall and has a diameter of 7.7m. It's thought to be around 2000 years old.

Page 7
PHOTOGRAPHER
David Clapp | Getty Images

The Milky Way.
The Dolomites, Italy

Home to our solar system, the mighty Milky Way contains more than 200 billion stars and perhaps almost as many planets – not least of which is Earth.

Page 8
PHOTOGRAPHER
Anita Stizzoli | Getty Images

Sulphuric lakes at Dallol.
Danakil Desert, Ethiopia

The ancient volcanic crater in Dallol creates amazing heat (it is said to be the hottest place on earth), colourful, acidic ponds, mountains of sulphur, and an out-of-this-world landscape.

Page 9
PHOTOGRAPHER
Radius Images | Corbis

Stone pinnacles at Cavusin.
Cappadocia, Turkey

Cappadocia is a geological oddity of honeycombed hills and towering boulders that were fashioned through volcanic ash and moulded by millennia of rain and river flow.

Page 10
PHOTOGRAPHER
George Steinmetz | Corbis

Moai (statues).
Easter Island, Pacific Ocean

The monolithic human figures on Easter Island were carved by the Rapa Nui people sometime between the years 1250 and 1500. The tallest statue is almost 10m high.

Page 11
PHOTOGRAPHER
Science Photo Library | Getty Images

Canyonlands National Park.
Utah, USA

Dawn's warm light hits the rock formations of Canyonlands. The arches, bridges, needles, spires and craters of Utah's largest park were carved by the Colorado River.

Page 12
PHOTOGRAPHER
Neale Clarke | Getty Images

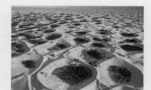

Adjder oasis.
Sahara Desert, Algeria

Water lies about 15m below the Adjder oasis, and the local farmers reach it via hand-dug wells. These days electric pumps make the task a lot easier.

Page 14
PHOTOGRAPHER
George Steinmetz | Corbis

Rice terraces at Yuanyuang.
Yunnan, China

In the southwest of China lies this fertile plateau of rice paddies. Agriculture in east Asia began 10,000 years ago, and prompted people to settle in one area.

Page 15
PHOTOGRAPHER
Panorama Media | Getty Images

Grand Canyon in the Blue Mountains.
New South Wales, Australia

The Blue Mountains National Park, 80km west of Sydney, comprises waterfalls, canyons and rainforest. An ancient tree species, the Wollemi pine, was found in a gorge here.

Page 16
PHOTOGRAPHER
Ted Mead | Getty Images

Ghoubbet-el-Kharab.
Djibouti

The fractures in the lava of Ghoubbet-el-Kharab – the Devil's Throat – continue to widen each year because of the high seismic activity; the region straddles three tectonic plates.

Page 17
PHOTOGRAPHER
Nigel Pavitt | Corbis

Plitvice Lakes National Park.
Croatia

This Unesco World Heritage–listed park is made up of interlinked and cascading lakes, caves and forest. The colours of the lakes range from azure to green, blue and even grey.

Page 18
PHOTOGRAPHER
Kelly Cheng | Getty Images

Boab trees.
Western Australia

These bulbous trees live throughout the Kimberley. For Australia's indigenous people they were a source of food, water and shelter.

Page 19
PHOTOGRAPHER
Peter Walton | Getty Images

Altocumulus clouds.
Amboseli National Park, Kenya

In some years the rains don't arrive in Amboseli National Park and one of Africa's best places to see wildlife becomes a desert; in other years heavy rains turn it into a swamp.

Page 20
PHOTOGRAPHER
Gerry Ellis | Getty Images

Fly geyser, Black Rock Desert.
Nevada, USA

While drilling for water in 1916, farmers struck a geothermal pocket of water; dissolved minerals accumulated to create colourful growths around the geyser.

Page 21
PHOTOGRAPHER
Theodore Clutter | Getty Images

The Bungle Bungles.
Purnululu National Park, Western Australia

The beehive-like landscape of the Bungle Bungles was formed by millions of years' worth of wind and rain. The distinctive mounds are striped with orange, black and grey bands.

Page 22
PHOTOGRAPHER
David Wall Photo | Getty Images

Kilauea volcano.
Hawaii, USA

Kilauea has erupted repeatedly since 1823, the year of the volcano's first well-documented eruption. Its lava splashes into the ocean and creates a new coastline.

Page 24
PHOTOGRAPHER
Toshi Sasaki | Getty Images

Lava at Kalapana.
Hawaii, USA

In the late 1980s and early 1990s lava flow invaded and destroyed the Hawaiian town of Kalapana. The landscape continues to change from day to day.

Page 25
PHOTOGRAPHER
Frank Krahmer | Corbis

Waterfall at Mýrdalsjökull glacier.
Iceland

The icecap of Mýrdalsjökull covers an active volcano, and the runoff from the glacier creates an impressively powerful waterfall.

Page 26
PHOTOGRAPHER
Thorsten Henn | Getty Images

Grand Canyon National Park.
Arizona, USA

The Grand Canyon is vast and nearly incomprehensible in age – it took six million years for the canyon to form and some rocks exposed along its walls are two billion years old.

Page 29
PHOTOGRAPHER
Universal Images Group | Getty Images

South Downs National Park.
West Sussex, England

An area of outstanding beauty, the South Downs is England's newest national park. The area is home to more than 110,000 people and is composed of working farmland and chalk hills.

Page 30
PHOTOGRAPHER
Slawek Staszczuk | Getty Images

Okavango River.
Botswana

The Okavango changes with the seasons as flood waters ebb and flow, creating islands, river channels and pathways for animals that move this way and that at the waters' behest.

Page 31
PHOTOGRAPHER
Cedric Favero | Getty Images

The Sardine Run.
Eastern Cape, South Africa

During the annual migration of sardines, millions of the fish head north along the coast of South Africa, creating a feeding frenzy along the way. The migration occurs from May to July.

Page 32
PHOTOGRAPHER
Dmitry Miroshnikov | Getty Images

Esis River Gorge.
New Britain Island, Papua New Guinea

Papua New Guinea is one of the least explored and least developed nations on earth; most people survive by subsistence farming, thanks to the abundant water.

Page 34
PHOTOGRAPHER
Stephen Alvarez | Getty Images

Fruit trees at Pessines.
Charente-Maritime, France

The wine-growing region of Charente-Maritime produces the Cognac variety of brandy and the French aperitif, Pineau des Charentes.

Page 35
PHOTOGRAPHER
Leroy Francis | Getty Images

Elephant.
Masai Mara, Kenya

The sweeping savannah of the Masai Mara is the place for the world's most spectacular display of wildlife. The drama is at its most intense in August, the start of the wildebeest migration.

Page 36
PHOTOGRAPHER
Andy Rouse | Corbis

Elephant herd.
Al-Sudd Swamp, South Sudan

Formed by the White Nile, the Al-Sudd is a vast swamp the size of England, and the largest such habitat in Africa.

Page 37
PHOTOGRAPHER
Mike D Kock | Getty Images

Steller's sea eagles.
Kamchatka, Russia

Steller's sea eagles thrive on a diet of salmon, and in the shallow, icy streams of Kamchatka they often find the fish frozen near the surface.

Page 38
PHOTOGRAPHER
Sergey Gorshkov | Getty Images

Rice terraces.
Longsheng, China

Terraced paddy fields wind up from the riverside to the mountain top in a feat of farm engineering that allows the communities of Longsheng to harvest rice in a mountainous area.

Page 39
PHOTOGRAPHER
KingWu | Getty Images

Umm al-Maa lake.
Ubari Sand Sea, Libya

Surrounded by sand, the Umm al-Maa (or Mother of Water) is a refreshing oasis in the Libyan desert. The lake is fed by natural springs, which have slowly been drying up.

Page 40
PHOTOGRAPHER
George Steinmetz | Corbis

Incahuasi Island.
Salar de Uyuni, Bolivia

The hilly outpost of Incahuasi Island is covered in Trichocereus cacti and surrounded by a flat white sea of hexagonal salt tiles. The salty expanse is an evocative and eerie sight.

Page 42
PHOTOGRAPHER
Juergen Ritterbach | Getty Images

Li River.
Guangxi Zhuang, China

The Li River area is renowned for classic images of mossy-green jagged limestone peaks, bubbling streams, wallowing water buffalo and cormorant fishing.

Page 43
PHOTOGRAPHER
GlowingEarth | Getty Images

Buffalo at Yellowstone National Park.
Wyoming, USA

More than 3000 buffalo roam throughout the Yellowstone National Park in Wyoming; they are among the last wild buffalo in the United States.

Page 44
PHOTOGRAPHER
Jeff Vanuga | Corbis

Plateau de Valensole.
Alpes de Haute-Provence, France

Lavender from the fields of the Plateau de Valensole is made into lavender oil, honey, soap and scented sachets. The lavender fields usually bloom in July.

Page 46
PHOTOGRAPHER
Altrendo Nature | Getty Images

Lyth Valley in the Lake District.
Cumbria, England

The unspoilt Lyth Valley is tucked in a hidden corner of Cumbria, where trees are laden with fruit and rolling hills are the most magnificent green.

Page 47
PHOTOGRAPHER
221A | Getty Images

Humpback whales in Chatham Strait.
Alaska, USA

The humpback whales in Chatham Strait spend their summers feeding on the healthy supply of krill and small bait fish that live in the waters.

Page 48
PHOTOGRAPHER
Kevin Schafer | Getty Images

Puffins.
The Shiant Isles, Scotland

Each year during spring and summer, millions of puffins set up home on the coasts of the Scottish archipelagos St Kilda and the Shiant Isles.

Page 50
PHOTOGRAPHER
Jim Richardson | Getty Images

Hippopotamus with egret.
Serengeti National Park, Tanzania

The Serengeti National Park regularly sees wildebeest stampeding across the plains, hippos jostling for space in rivers and elephants kicking up the dust.

Page 51
PHOTOGRAPHER
Gerry Ellis | Getty Images

Electrical storm.
Saskatchewan, Canada

When Saskatchewan's plains heat up in the afternoon, rising hot air which then cools rapidly causes thunderstorms with lightning bolts that can be hotter than the sun's surface.

Page 52
PHOTOGRAPHER
Dave Reede | Getty Images

The Na Pali coast of Kaua'i.
Hawaii, USA

For six million years the Pacific Ocean's waves have broken on Kaua'i's volcanic shores. The Na Pali coast in the northwest is a State Wilderness Park, attracting hikers and kayakers.

Page 54
PHOTOGRAPHER
Laura Barisonzi | Corbis

Surfing Phantoms at O'ahu.
Hawaii, USA

Surfing was redefined in Hawaii in 2000 when riders began to be towed into monstrous waves by jet skis. Phantoms is a reef break on O'ahu's north shore.

Page 55
PHOTOGRAPHER
Sean Davey | Getty Images

Eyjafjallajökull volcano.
Iceland

The 2010 eruption of this volcano, on Iceland's south coast, blew volcanic ash many kilometres into the atmosphere. It's now considered dormant, once again.

Page 56
PHOTOGRAPHER
Jon Vidar Sigurdsson | Getty Images

Nideck waterfall.
Alsace, France

The waterfall at Nideck is set in a forest, beneath a castle. The castle appears in a story by the Grimm brothers about giants, and in winter the frozen falls add to the fairytale scene.

Page 57
PHOTOGRAPHER
Philippe Sainte-Laudy | Getty Images

Freshwater lagoons.
Lençóis Maranhenses National Park, Brazil

Freshwater lagoons are formed when these low-lying sand dunes are flooded during the Amazon basin's rainy season. But despite the water, very little vegetation survives here.

Page 58
PHOTOGRAPHER
George Steinmetz | Corbis

Iceberg arch.
Antarctica

One of the reasons why icebergs float is that they contain a lot of air. Another reason is that they're formed from freshwater, which is less dense that salty water.

Page 60
PHOTOGRAPHER
kajophotography.com | Getty Images

Ta Prohm temple.
Angkor Wat, Cambodia

Ta Prohm was built 800 years ago but was abandoned in the 17th century after the fall of the Khmer empire. Over subsequent centuries the jungle reclaimed the ruins.

Page 61
PHOTOGRAPHER
Ignacio Ayestaran | Getty Images

Lake Baikal.
Siberia, Russia

The world's deepest freshwater lake is perhaps also its oldest, at up to 30 million years of age. It's fed by 330 rivers, which descend off the surrounding mountains.

Page 62
PHOTOGRAPHER
James Morgan | Corbis

Svartifoss.
Vatnajökull National Park, Iceland

The basalt columns of this waterfall in southeast Iceland inspired Reykjavík's Hallgrímskirkja, Iceland's largest church.

Page 63
PHOTOGRAPHER
Snorri Gunnarsson | Getty Images

Cypresses in Henderson Lake.
Louisiana, USA

Life around the wetlands and bayous of Louisiana proceeds at its own pace; the region has its own music, its own food and its own way of doing things.

Page 64
PHOTOGRAPHER
Frank Krahmer | Getty Images

Icelandic horses.
Iceland

Occupying the space between wild and domesticated, Iceland's iconic purebred horses roam free every summer and are rounded up at the end of the season.

Page 66
PHOTOGRAPHER
Martin Sundberg | Corbis

Condors.
Colca Canyon, Peru

In one of the world's deepest canyons, Andean condors use their 3m-wide wingspan to soar on rising currents of air, watching out for carrion below.

Page 67
PHOTOGRAPHER
B Holland | Getty Images

The Devil's Washbowl on Malad River.
Idaho, USA

The flow of the Malad River, a tributary of the Snake River in the American northwest, is controlled by dams and reservoirs. But it's still a wild ride when in full flow.

Page 68
PHOTOGRAPHER
Mark Weber | Getty Images

Lava from Kilauea volcano.
Hawaii, USA

Kilauea, one of the world's most active volcanoes, has been erupting continuously since 1983. Hawaii is thought to sit on a hotspot rather than the edge of a tectonic plate.

Page 69
PHOTOGRAPHER
G Brad Lewis | Getty Images

Pinware River.
Labrador, Canada

The Pinware is a famous salmon-fishing river; each river in North America had its own strain of salmon, though they are now diluted by farmed and reintroduced stock.

Page 70
PHOTOGRAPHER
Shaun Lowe | Getty Images

Torres del Paine National Park.
Patagonia, Chile

The 'horns' of Torres del Paine are the centrepiece of this rugged Andean park at the southern tip of Chile. The weather here can be diabolical at any time of the year.

Page 71
PHOTOGRAPHER
Luis Davilla | Getty Images

Zebras.
NamibRand Nature Reserve, Namibia

NamibRand is one of the largest private reserves in Southern Africa and is home to both Hartman's and Burchell's zebras, plus oryx, springbok and leopards.

Page 72
PHOTOGRAPHER
George Steinmetz | Corbis

Iguazú Falls.
Brazil–Argentina border

Islands split the 2.7km-wide waterfall into numerous cataracts – one of them is called the Devil's Throat, across which the border between Brazil and Argentina lies.

Page 74
PHOTOGRAPHER
KTSFotos | Getty Images

The Tarkine wilderness.
Tasmania, Australia

In northwest Tasmania, the Tarkine is an important area of cool-temperate rainforest – a throwback to Gondwana, the super-continent that fractured to create the southern hemisphere.

Page 75
PHOTOGRAPHER
Peter Walton | Getty Images

Great White shark.
Gaudalupe Island, Mexico

From the day they hatch, Great White sharks have to remain in perpetual motion so oxygenated water flows over their gills. An adult will eat 11 tons of food per year.

Page 76
PHOTOGRAPHER
Norbert Wu | Corbis

Avalanche.
Rhône-Alpes, France

Avalanche prediction is more art than science, with snow types and weather patterns causing unstable layers of snow. When the snow does let go, it can fall at 130km/h.

Page 77
PHOTOGRAPHER
Marco Maccarini | Getty Images

Ogimachi village.
Gifu, Japan

In Shirakawa-go, deep in central Japan's mountains, the traditional farmhouses had steep roofs to withstand the heavy snows. The loft was used to cultivate silk worms.

Page 79
PHOTOGRAPHER
Agustin Rafael C Reyes | Getty Images

Beni Isguen.
Ghardaïa, Algeria

In Algeria's Saharan M'Zab region, this 14th-century religious settlement retains its traditions and has changed little over the centuries. Visitors are permitted only with a local guide.

Page 80
PHOTOGRAPHER
George Steinmetz | Corbis

The Great Barrier Reef.
Queensland, Australia

The world's most extensive coral reef system supports 1500 species of fish and 4000 types of mollusc, each dependent on another. It's the most biodiverse of Unesco's World Heritage sites.

Page 81
PHOTOGRAPHER
George Steinmetz | Corbis

Manhattan.
New York, USA

At almost 40,000 people per sq km in 1910, Manhattan's population density was higher then than in 2010. But at today's median price of US$800,000 for an apartment, the cost of property has gone up.

Page 82
PHOTOGRAPHER
Nikada | Getty Images

Water buffalo.
Ban Gioc, Vietnam

The waterfall at Ban Gioc, on Vietnam's border with China, has long been the focal point of the local community, somewhere livestock can be washed and watered.

Page 84
PHOTOGRAPHER
HNH Images | Getty Images

King penguins.
Antarctica

King penguins congregrate to raise their chicks, herding the young birds together to protect them from the cold. The chicks take up to 10 months to fledge.

Page 86
PHOTOGRAPHER
DLILLC | Corbis

Green turtles.
Galápagos Islands, Ecuador

To lay their eggs, Green turtles often return to the exact beach where they hatched. Just 1% of hatchlings will reach maturity to repeat the cycle.

Page 88
PHOTOGRAPHER
Paul Kennedy | Getty Images

Red deer in Richmond Park.
London, England

Introduced in the 16th century to entertain royal hunting parties, red deer still roam relatively freely in Richmond Park. The rutting season, when males compete, starts in September.

Page 89
PHOTOGRAPHER
Alex Saberi | Getty Images

Halong Bay.
Gulf of Tonkin, Vietnam

Evidence suggests Halong Bay's 500-million-year-old limestone islands have been a home to people for 20,000 years; today, four fishing villages support up to 2000 people.

Page 90
PHOTOGRAPHER
Bruno De Hogues | Getty Images

Monarch Butterfly Biosphere Reserve.
Michoacán, Mexico

Each winter one billion butterflies flap 4000 km across North America to this reserve in Mexico. The journey exceeds the insect's lifespan; no one knows how different generations return to the same location.

Page 92
PHOTOGRAPHER
Education Images/UIG | Getty Images

Manarola town in Cinque Terre.
Liguria, Italy

The five villages of the Italian Riviera date back centuries, when locals grew grapes, caught fish and dreaded pirate attacks. Today sightseers are the source of income.

Page 93
PHOTOGRAPHER
Gianluca Giardi | Getty Images

A water hole in Etosha National Park.
Namibia

Where there's water, animals in Africa can't be fussy about the company they keep; giraffes, zebras, kudus and namaqua sandgrouse take a drink in arid Etosha National Park.

Page 94
PHOTOGRAPHER
Frans Lanting | Getty Images

Bartaga village.
Niger River, Mali

The delta of the Niger River, on the edge of the Sahara, supports two million people in Mali but the water is under threat from industrial agriculture.

Page 96
PHOTOGRAPHER
George Steinmetz | Corbis

Sun City.
Arizona, USA

Launched in the 1960s, Sun City is a modern town popular with retirees. Creating a sense of community in ever-increasing suburbia is a challenge for urban planners.

Page 97
PHOTOGRAPHER
Randy Wells | Getty Images

Flamingos.
Lake Turkana, Kenya

The world's largest alkaline lake lies on the border with Ethiopia. Its plankton supports a population of Greater flamingos and lends the birds their pink hue.

Page 98
PHOTOGRAPHER
Michael Poliza | Getty Images

Vidigal favela.
Rio de Janeiro, Brazil

This neighbourhood overlooks Ipanema beach. Once plagued by gang wars, it is gradually gentrifying, with an influx of incomers bringing new pressures.

Page 100
PHOTOGRAPHER
luoman | Getty Images

The village of Reine.
Lofoten Islands, Norway

The fishermen's cottages on the Lofoten Islands, an Arctic archipelago, provided shelter between winter fishing trips; the catch was dried during the summer.

Page 101
PHOTOGRAPHER
Olaf Krüger | Corbis

Bluebell wood.
Hampshire, England

The deciduous woods of southern England are filled with the scent of these graceful, dark-blue flowers in May. England has around half the world's population of bluebells.

Page 102
PHOTOGRAPHER
David Clapp | Getty Images

Callanish standing stones.
Isle of Lewis, Scotland

More beautiful than Stonehenge and with less restricted access, the Callanish stone circle is the perfect place to celebrate the summer solstice. It was constructed almost 5000 years ago.

Page 104
PHOTOGRAPHER
Patrick Dieudonne | Corbis

Mani Rimdu festival.
Sagarmatha, Nepal

During this 19-day Buddhist festival, held across Himalayan Nepal, monks perform rituals before a three-day public festival begins. It takes place in the 10th month of the Tibetan lunar calendar.

Page 105
PHOTOGRAPHER
Richard I'Anson | Getty Images

Cherry blossom.
Yuantouzhu, China

It's not just Japan that reveres cherry blossom; when hundreds of the trees burst into flower on Yuantouzhu, a peninsula at Lake Tai, visitors arrive to savour the sight.

Page 106
PHOTOGRAPHER
200 | Getty Images

Xoxo cemetery.
Oaxaca, Mexico

The Day of the Dead, a blend of Catholicism and ancient Aztec rituals, is a joyous occasion, celebrating the lives of loved ones. It takes place in early November.

Page 108
PHOTOGRAPHER
Kenneth Garrett | Corbis

Black-browed albatross.
South Georgia Island, Atlantic Ocean

Black-browed albatrosses tend to mate for life, returning every year of their life – which may be as long as 30 years – to the same colony in the South Atlantic.

Page 109
PHOTOGRAPHER
Frans Lanting | Corbis

Holi festival.
India

The Hindu spring festival Holi takes place with an explosion of colour across India, but especially in Gujarat. It celebrates the fertility of the land.

Page 110
PHOTOGRAPHER
Poras Chaudhary | Getty Images

The Sardine Run.
Eastern Cape, South Africa

When billions of sardines spawn then swim north up the South African coast, predators such as these Common dolphins arrive to pick up an easy meal.

Page 112
PHOTOGRAPHER
Rainer Schimpf | Getty Images

Lantern festival.
Chiang Mai, Thailand

Yi Peng, Chiang Mai's version of the Thai festival Loi Krathong, takes place during a full moon in November and sees lanterns launched into the night sky.

Page 114
PHOTOGRAPHER
Athit Perawongmetha | Getty Images

Snow geese and sandhill cranes.
New Mexico, USA

Sandhill cranes and snow geese pass the winter at Bosque del Apache National Wildlife Refuge on the Rio Grande. Each morning they fly in and then fly out in the evening.

Page 116
PHOTOGRAPHER
Ralph Clevenger | Corbis

Polar bear.
Churchill, Canada

Pregnant polar bears retreat to a den to give birth during winter, but most polar bears shake off winter by entering a state of 'walking hibernation' when they may not eat for weeks.

Page 117
PHOTOGRAPHER
Cordier Sylvain | Getty Images

Vineyards in Greve.
Tuscany, Italy

Romans, and before them the Etruscans, cultivated vines like these in Chianti. Wine wasn't reserved for special occasions; a daily allowance was recommended.

Page 118
PHOTOGRAPHER
Massimo Ripani | Corbis

Danum Valley Conservation Area.
Borneo, Malaysia

This important parcel of lowland forest in Sabah is home to some of Malaysia's rarest creatures, including orang-utans and pygmy elephants.

Page 120
PHOTOGRAPHER
Frans Lanting | Corbis

The Austfonna ice cap.
Svalbard, Norway

High up at the tip of Svalbard, on the edge of the Arctic Ocean, lies the largest ice cap in Europe. It has a maximum thickness of more than 500m, which thins a little during the summer.

Page 123
PHOTOGRAPHER
Andy Rouse | Getty Images

The Dolomites.
South Tyrol, Italy

Millions of years ago the pale peaks and pinnacles of the Dolomites lay on the seabed; now they are among the world's most distinctive mountainscapes.

Page 124
PHOTOGRAPHER
Michele Galli | Getty Images

Monument Valley Tribal Park.
Arizona–Utah, USA

The sandstone spires of Monument Valley, part of the Colorado Plateau, are the result of millions of years of erosion. Iron oxide gives the rock its reddish tone.

Page 126
PHOTOGRAPHER
Ron and Patty Thomas Photography | Getty Images

Reed Flute Cave.
Guangxi, China

The limestone stalactites and stalagmites of this cave in Guilin have formed drip by drip over more than 100 million years. They're illuminated for sightseers.

Page 127
PHOTOGRAPHER
Loco Moco Photos | Getty Images

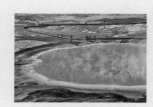

Yellowstone National Park.
Wyoming, USA

The colours of the Grand Prismatic Spring, the largest hot spring in the USA, derive from different types of bacteria that each thrive in a certain temperature of water.

Page 128
PHOTOGRAPHER
Noppawat | Getty Images

Francois Peron National Park.
Western Australia

Western Australia's desert meets the Pacific Ocean at Cape Lesueur. This finger of land protects the fragile coastline lying behind it from erosion.

Page 130
PHOTOGRAPHER
Rachel Lewis | Getty Images

Wildflowers in the Mojave Desert.
California, USA

After rain falls, the Dumont Dunes bloom with flowers such as sand verbena and dune primrose. Desert plants quickly exploit any water.

Page 131
PHOTOGRAPHER
Christopher Talbot Frank | Corbis

The Black Forest.
Baden-Württemberg, Germany

In the southwest of Germany, winter turns the Black Forest's trees white and cross-country skiers and snowshoe-wearing hikers take to the trails.

Page 132
PHOTOGRAPHER
Daniel Schoenen | Getty Images

Drakes Passage.
Southern Ocean, Antarctica

Named in English after 16th-century sailor Sir Francis Drake, this is the tumultuous stretch of water between Antarctica and South America; it was closed until 41 million years ago.

Page 133
PHOTOGRAPHER
Mike Hill | Getty Images

The aurora borealis.
Kiruna, Sweden

When charged particles, which flow from the sun at 1.4 million km/h, hit the Earth's magnetic field at the planet's poles, they create curtains of light. Solar storms heighten the effect.

Page 134
PHOTOGRAPHER
Antony Spencer | Getty Images

Zhangye Danxia Landform Geological Park.
Gansu, China

In northwest China, the colourful stripes of this rock formation come from the red sandstone and minerals, which date back 24 million years.

Page 136
PHOTOGRAPHER
Fu Chunrong | Corbis

Nashua River.
New Hampshire, USA

The trees of the northeast USA have some of the most spectacular displays of autumn foliage when chlorophyll retreats from their leaves as days get colder and darker.

Page 137
PHOTOGRAPHER
George Steinmetz | Corbis

Bora Bora.
French Polynesia, Pacific Ocean

Once an extinct volcano, Bora Bora is the most famous of the Leeward Islands in the South Pacific. Tropical fish swim in the lagoon formed by its outer rim.

Page 138
PHOTOGRAPHER
Mint Images | Getty Images

A supercell storm near Alvo.
Nebraska, USA

Supercell thunderstorms have a powerful, rotating updraft. They're prevalent across a strip of the USA's Great Plains known as Tornado Alley.

Page 140
PHOTOGRAPHER
Mike Hollingshead | Getty Images

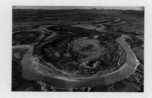

Gates of the Arctic National Park and Preserve.
Alaska, USA

At the North Fork of the Koyukuk River, a tributary of the Yukon, the water is slowly carving an oxbow lake. Part of its floodplain is a wetland wildlife reserve, especially popular with moose.

Page 141
PHOTOGRAPHER
Michael Melford | Getty Images

Iceberg in Grandidier Channel.
Pleneau Island, Antarctica

Although Grandidier Channel is one of the navigable channels of Antartica, mariners have to beware of icebergs, 40,000 of which are calved every year.

Page 142
PHOTOGRAPHER
Allan White | Getty Images

Slot canyon.
Utah, USA

Utah's sandstone plateaus are sliced by thousands of slot canyons, formed when a crack in the rock is forced wider by swirling water, eddying around imperfections.

Page 143

PHOTOGRAPHER
Michelle McCarron | Getty Images

Eyjafjallajökull volcano.
Iceland

Electrical storms are not uncommon when a volcano erupts explosively – they are generated by charged particles of volcanic ash.

Page 144

PHOTOGRAPHER
Arctic-Images | Corbis

Grand Canyon.
Arizona, USA

The current Grand Canyon is just six million years old. As canyons age they get broader and deeper; the Grand Canyon is getting deeper each year by the thickness of a sheet of paper.

Page 145

PHOTOGRAPHER
franckreporter | Getty Images

Skógafoss.
Iceland

This is one of the largest of Iceland's many waterfalls, thanks to the island's abundant rain and rivers. The spray from Skógafoss often creates a rainbow.

Page 146

PHOTOGRAPHER
Peerakit JIrachetthakun | Getty Images

Camel caravan.
Fachi, Niger

West Africa's Tuareg traders run camel caravans during the winter through Niger's Ténéré Desert, carrying salt and enough food for the camels.

Page 148

PHOTOGRAPHER
George Steinmetz | Corbis

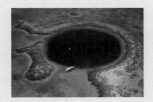

Lighthouse Reef.
Belize

At 125m deep, Belize's Great Blue Hole isn't bottomless but the sinkhole is connected to an extended series of underwater caves formed in the limestone tens of thousands of years ago.

Page 150

PHOTOGRAPHER
Schafer & Hill | Getty Images

Milford Sound.
Fiordland National Park, New Zealand

This is a place of superlatives, where the rainfall is measured in metres and the waterfalls are among the world's tallest. Milford Sound's walls extend 1200m upwards.

Page 151

PHOTOGRAPHER
Frans Lemmens | Corbis

Neversink Pit.
Alabama, USA

Open-air caves, known as pits in the USA and potholes in the UK, pepper Tennessee, Alabama and Georgia. Neversink is a classic example, its fern-lined walls sinking 50m into Jackson County.

Page 152

PHOTOGRAPHER
George Steinmetz | Corbis

Seljalandsfoss.
Iceland

There are many waterfalls in Iceland but Seljalandsfoss's claim to fame is that visitors can venture behind it. It is just off the southern Ring Road.

Page 154

PHOTOGRAPHER
Pétur Reynisson | Getty Images

A cenote near Valladolid.
Yucatán, Mexico

There are thousands of these water-filled, subterranean chambers in the Yucatán; the water comes from rain slowly filtering through the ground.

Page 155

PHOTOGRAPHER
ML Sinibaldi | Corbis

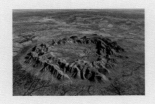

Meteorite crater at Gosse Bluff.
Northern Territory, Australia

Thought to be the result of an asteroid impact in the heart of Australia, just west of Alice Springs, the edges of this crater have been eroded over time.

Page 156

PHOTOGRAPHER
Frans Lanting | Getty Images

Mt Civetta.
The Dolomites, Italy

The great walls of Mt Civetta frame the town of Alleghe, in northern Italy. In this three-dimensional playground rock climbers test their skills.

Page 158

PHOTOGRAPHER
Alberto Simonetti | Getty Images

Hammerhead sharks.
Galápagos Islands, Ecuador

Under the oceans' surface, strange phenomena can be seen, including large gatherings of Scalloped Hammerhead sharks. At night the sharks disperse to forage for food.

Page 160

PHOTOGRAPHER
Chris Newbert | Getty Images

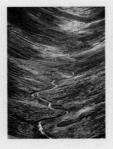

Wrangell–St Elias Wilderness.
Alaska, USA

Bulldozed by glaciers during the last ice age, the valleys of the Wrangell–St Elias Wilderness are part of the largest national park in the USA.

Page 162

PHOTOGRAPHER
Frans Lanting | Getty Images

Oneonta Creek, Columbia River Gorge.
Oregon, USA

So narrow that hikers wading the creek can touch both walls, the Oneonta Gorge is home to a variety of ferns and mosses that grow only in this corner of Oregon.

Page 163

PHOTOGRAPHER
Greg Vaughn | Corbis

Victoria Harbour.
Hong Kong

Hong Kong is one of the most densely populated cities in the world and as a result it has one of the highest rates of public transport usage in the world.

Page 164
PHOTOGRAPHER
Gavin Hellier | Corbis

Bracken cave. **Texas, USA**

At dusk, in summer, Mexican free-tailed bats pour from the 60m-wide mouth of this cave – all 20 million of them. It's the world's largest bat colony; 500 baby bats have been counted clinging to an expanse of wall smaller than this closed book.

Page 166
PHOTOGRAPHER
Michael Durham | Corbis

Migrating buffalo.
Moremi Game Reserve, Botswana

Botswana's buffalo move across the Okavango Delta's wetlands and savannah in search of food, closely followed by prides of lions that prey on them.

Page 167
PHOTOGRAPHER
Chris Harvey | Getty Images

Tasiilaq.
Greenland

On the east coast of Greenland, just 100km south of the Arctic Circle, Tasiilaq is home to about 2000 people. The sea on its doorstep freezes in the winter.

Page 168
PHOTOGRAPHER
Peter Adams | Corbis

Hadrian's Wall.
Northumberland, England

Built in AD122 to keep barbarous northerners out of Roman Britain, Hadrian's Wall was one of the most fortified borders of the time. Today it lies entirely within England.

Page 170
PHOTOGRAPHER
Rod Edwards | Getty Images

Sossusvlei sand dunes.
Namibia

The older the sand dunes in the Namib-Naukluft National Park, the redder they are. The Sossusvlei's dunes can reach 200m in height and they collect dew from the neighbouring ocean.

Page 171
PHOTOGRAPHER
D Lepp George | Getty Images

Cypresses in the Val d'Orcia.
Tuscany, Italy

Etruscans planted cypresses (actually from Persia or Syria) around their burial grounds because the trees kept their leaves in winter and were fragrant.

Page 172
PHOTOGRAPHER
Peter Zelei | Getty Images

Pura Ulun Danu
Bratan temple.
Bali, Indonesia

Built in the 17th century to honour the water goddess Dewi Danu, this is one of Bali's most important temples. Traditionally, Bali has relied on irrigation for its agriculture.

Page 174
PHOTOGRAPHER
Anders Blomqvist | Getty Images

The Devil's Marbles in
Tennant Creek.
Northern Territory, Australia

There are balancing stones all over the world, from Hampi in India to the southwest of the USA. These ancient stones in Australia are formed from granite that has weathered.

Page 175
PHOTOGRAPHER
Peter Walton Photography | Getty Images

Central Park in Manhattan.
New York, USA

During the 19th century, Central Park was carefully sculpted; swamps were drained and topsoil imported from New Jersey. It wasn't until the 1960s that cars were banned from the park at weekends.

Page 176
PHOTOGRAPHER
Michael Yamashita | Corbis

Red-crowned cranes.
Hokkaido, Japan

The rare red-crowned cranes of Hokkaido, of which there are about 1000, dance in pairs throughout the year, reinforcing the pair's bonds. The local Ainu people call them 'the gods of the marshes'.

Page 178
PHOTOGRAPHER
Panorama Media | Getty Images

Red-crowned cranes.
Hokkaido, Japan

The cranes' dances include bowing, jumping, synchronised strutting and the tossing of grass and sticks. To the Japanese the cranes symbolise luck and longevity.

Page 179
PHOTOGRAPHER
Piterpan | Getty Images

Triglav National Park.
Slovenia

Slovenia's only national park fans out around the country's highest peak, Mt Triglav. This land of forests and crystalline lakes in the Eastern Julian Alps is bordered by Italy and Austria.

Page 180
PHOTOGRAPHER
Guy Edwardes | Getty Images

Inuit hunter.
Qaanaaq, Greenland

Nothing from a successful Inuit hunting trip goes to waste: meat is eaten by people and animals, and the skins are used for warmth, shelter and to make kayaks.

Page 182
PHOTOGRAPHER
Louise Murray | Getty Images

Mustering horses.
Xilin Gol, Mongolia

Mongolia's xilingol horse is not wild but the breed is at home on the vast grasslands and is used for riding and work.

Page 183
PHOTOGRAPHER
TAO Images Limited | Getty Images

Tsingy de Bemaraha
Strict Nature Reserve.
Madagascar

Animals – including lemurs such as the sifaka – and plants have evolved to live among the jagged pinnacles (tsingys) of this park in the west of Madagascar. The reserve was founded in 1998.

Page 184
PHOTOGRAPHER
Yann Arthus-Bertrand | Corbis

Moraine Lake in Banff
National Park.
Alberta, Canada

Moraine Lake, fed by glacial waters, is overlooked by the Valley of the Ten Peaks. The peaks range from 3000m to 3400m. Mt Allen is named after the cartographer who mapped the region.

Page 185
PHOTOGRAPHER
Matt Champlin | Getty Images

Highland cattle.
Scotland

Scotland's distinctive Highland cattle were bred to survive cold weather and to forage for food in a harsh landscape. Despite appearances, they're very mild-mannered.

Page 186
PHOTOGRAPHER
Jan Vermeer| Corbis

The Cuillins.
Isle of Skye, Scotland

The wild Black Cuillins of this island in the Inner Hebrides draw climbers and hikers from far and wide. The island is home to golden eagles and red deer.

Page 187
PHOTOGRAPHER
Julian Calverley | Corbis

The Kimberley coast.
Western Australia

The coastline of this vast and hitherto unspoiled wilderness extends 1300km and is home to the world's largest population of humpback whales.

Page 188
PHOTOGRAPHER
Steve Parish | Corbis

A quiver tree.
**Kalahari, Namibia–
South Africa**

The quiver tree survives in its arid world by storing water in thick green leaves and fat white branches. It can self-amputate branches when conditions are exceptionally dry.

Page 190
PHOTOGRAPHER
Jaco Wolmarans | Getty Images

Kamakura Bamboo Garden.
Tokyo, Japan

Formal Japanese gardens were often designed for Zen-like meditation, with each plant selected for its aesthetic appeal; bamboo is sometimes used to hide features and create a sense of mystery.

Page 191
PHOTOGRAPHER
Marco Maccarini | Getty Images

Lamayuru monastery.
Ladakh, India

One of the oldest gompas (monasteries) in Western Ladakh, Lamayuru lies on the Srinagar–Leh road in Kargil district.

Page 192
PHOTOGRAPHER
Jaturong Kengwinit | Getty Images

Rice paddies.
Bali, Indonesia

Terraced fields allow rice to be grown on steep slopes and make irrigation easier. Ubud in central Bali is famed for this type of farming.

Page 194
PHOTOGRAPHER
Denis Waugh | Getty Images

Tianmen mountain road.
Hunan, China

It took eight years to build this 10km stretch of road in the Tianmen Mountain National Park, which is in the southeast of the country.

Page 195
PHOTOGRAPHER
Tom Horton | Getty Images

Wildebeest migration.
Masai Mara, Kenya

At 800km, it's not the world's longest migration but it is the largest in volume. Two million wildebeest move from the Serengeti to the Masai Mara, braving the crocodiles of the Mara River along the way.

Page 197
PHOTOGRAPHER
Anup Shah | Getty Images

Victoria Falls.
Zambia–Zimbabwe

At more than 1700m in width, Victoria Falls have the highest recorded volume of water tumbling over the edge: 12,800 cu metres per second. Peak flow is in April.

Page 198
PHOTOGRAPHER
Pascal Boegli | Getty Images

Bryce Canyon National Park.
Utah, USA

The Wall Street Trail of Bryce Canyon has its own skyscrapers: ponderosa pines. Chasms in the rock are formed when water freezes and expands, creating alleys up to 60m deep.

Page 200
PHOTOGRAPHER
Sarun Laowong | Getty Images

The Gasherbrum massif.
Karakorum, Pakistan

Part of the Gasherbrum massif on the border of Pakistan and China, 8035m Gasherbrum II was first summited in 1956. This photo was taken when Cory Richards and his team made a film here in 2011.

Page 201
PHOTOGRAPHER
Cory Richards | Getty Images

The Great Wall.
Huanghuacheng, China

The Great Wall is a conjunction of walls, initially constructed for defence and then to control immigration and levy taxes. The wall, restored by the Ming dynasty, extends 8850km.

Page 202
PHOTOGRAPHER
Bu Xiangdong | Corbis

Nabiyotum volcano.
Kenya

The circular crater of Nabiyotum stands in northern Kenya's Lake Turkana, the world's largest alkaline lake. The Great Rift Valley is home to a number of craters as well as still-active volcanoes.

Page 203

PHOTOGRAPHER
Nigel Pavitt | Getty Images

Angkor Wat.
Siem Reap, Cambodia

Angkor Wat is where the civic and the spiritual meet. The world's largest religious monument, 'the temple that is a city' was built by Khmer kings in the 12th century.

Page 204

PHOTOGRAPHER
Dozier Marc | Getty Images

Avenue of the Baobabs.
Morondava, Madagascar

These baobab trees would have once stood as part of a dense and diverse forest. This is the largest variety, Grandidier's baobab, and can store 120,000l in their 30m trunks.

Page 205

PHOTOGRAPHER
Vincent Grafhorst | Getty Images

Los Glaciares National Park.
Patagonia, Argentina

Mt Fitzroy to the right and spiky Cerro Torre to the left are the two landmark mountains in Patagonia's ice fields, the world's largest outside Antarctica.

Page 206

PHOTOGRAPHER
Colin Monteath | Getty Images

Whale shark.
Western Australia

The world's largest fish species has a particular fondness for Ningaloo Reef, off Western Australia, where it filters the water for plankton and tiny fish.

Page 208

PHOTOGRAPHER
Colin Parker | Corbis

Ningaloo Marine Park.
Western Australia

At places, it's possible to swim from the shore of Western Australia to the world's largest fringing reef, the Ningaloo, which is home to more than 500 species of fish, turtles and rays.

Page 209

PHOTOGRAPHER
Col Roberts | Getty Images

The Palace of Westminster.
London, England

After a fire that razed the Houses of Parliament in 1834, Sir Charles Barry redesigned the Palace of Westminster. Big Ben is the name of the bell, which tolls at the top of Elizabeth Tower.

Page 210

PHOTOGRAPHER
Enzo Figueres | Getty Images

Monument Valley.
Arizona–Utah, USA

Monument Valley's fame far exceeds its size thanks to roles in numerous movies. The 300m-high sandstone buttes have appeared in films as diverse as *Stagecoach* and *2001: A Space Odyssey*.

Page 210

PHOTOGRAPHER
Dan Ballard | Getty Images

Giraffes.
Okavango Delta, Botswana

Most rivers empty into an ocean but not landlocked Botswana's Okavango river. It floods a plain of 5000–15,000 sq km, creating a watery haven for wildlife large and small.

Page 212

PHOTOGRAPHER
Richard Du Toit | Getty Images

Millau Viaduct.
Midi-Pyrénées, France

The world's tallest bridge spans the valley of the River Tarn in southern France for 2460m. It cost €400 million to construct and is estimated to last 120 years.

Page 214

PHOTOGRAPHER
The Image Bank | Getty Images

Yosemite National Park.
California, USA

North America's highest measured waterfall, Yosemite Falls, cascades into the Merced River. Yosemite National Park covers 3000 sq km, though it is Yosemite Valley that draws the largest number of visitors.

Page 215

PHOTOGRAPHER
Doug Steakley | Getty Images

The Kogelberg coast.
Western Cape, South Africa

Kogelberg Nature Reserve, east of Cape Town, receives moisture-laden air from the South Atlantic. It has some of the greatest diversity of plant life in the world.

Page 216

PHOTOGRAPHER
Martin Harvey | Corbis

Strokkur geyser.
Iceland

The Strokkur geyser erupts every four to eight minutes, blasting water up to 40m into the air. The word 'geyser' itself comes from Icelandic, 'geysa', which means 'to gush'.

Page 218

PHOTOGRAPHER
ABG | Getty Images

Limestone pinnacles at Wulingyuan.
Hunan, China

The karst shards of Wulingyuan are what remain of quartzite sandstone mountains after millions of years of water erosion. They're part of Zhangjiajie National Forest Park.

Page 219

PHOTOGRAPHER
Feng Wei Photography | Getty Images

Angel Falls.
Venezuela

Jimmie Angel was an American aviator who flew over the world's tallest waterfall in 1933. He landed there in 1937 with his wife but his plane became stuck; they trekked for 11 days to reach safety.

Page 221

PHOTOGRAPHER
James Marshall | Corbis

The Royal Tomb at Petra.
Jordan

Petra's significance is due to its historic location between Arabia, Egypt and Syria-Phoenicia. The crossroads of trading routes was inhabited since prehistoric times.

Page 222

PHOTOGRAPHER
Wallacefsk | Getty Images

Pipeline, O'ahu.
Hawaii, USA

Crashing onto a body-shredding reef on Hawaii's north shore, Pipeline is believed to be the most dangerous wave in the world to surf.

Page 224

PHOTOGRAPHER
Kaz Mori | Getty Images

The Wave, Coyote Buttes.
Arizona–Utah, USA

Two effects are on display at this part of the Paria Canyon–Vermilion Cliffs Wilderness: the laying down of sediment under long-gone seas, and the wearing down of rock by the elements.

Page 225

PHOTOGRAPHER
Crisma | Getty Images

Uluru.
Northern Territory, Australia

Uluru is 335km southwest of Alice Springs in Australia's hot, red heart. It's formed from rock thought to have been deposited more than 500 million years ago, and it once lay on a sea's bed.

Page 226

PHOTOGRAPHER
Michael Dunning | Getty Images

Taj Mahal.
Uttar Pradesh, India

The Taj Mahal is a monument to love, composed in white marble – over 20 years from 1632 – to honour Mumtaz Mahal, wife of Mughal Emperor Shah Jahan.

Page 227

PHOTOGRAPHER
Frans Lemmens | Getty Images

Zabriskie Point, Death Valley.
California, USA

Death Valley was the bed of a lake millions of years ago. Its sediment created the stripes seen at Zabriskie; the dark layer is from five-million-year-old volcanic eruptions.

Page 228

PHOTOGRAPHER
Stephanie Sawyer | Getty Images

Terracotta Army, Xi'an.
Shaanxi, China

The Terracotta Army was buried with Emperor Qin Shi Huang in 210BC. The 8000 soldiers were to protect the emperor in the afterlife. He was also buried with musicians and acrobats.

Page 230

PHOTOGRAPHER
Tom Till | Getty Images

Terracotta Army, Xi'an.
Shaanxi, China

The figures in the Terracotta army were constructed in pieces, then assembled. They have different facial expressions and vary in height and uniform; their weapons were real.

Page 231

PHOTOGRAPHER
O Louis Mazzatenta | Getty Images

Shiprock.
New Mexico, USA

Rather than being a sandstone buttress, Shiprock is actually the eroded vestige of a volcanic plug, standing 2188m above the desert. The Navajo people wove many myths about its form.

Page 232

PHOTOGRAPHER
Wild Horizon | Getty Images

The Temple of Saturn.
Rome, Italy

Standing in ancient Rome's Forum, this temple was dedicated to Saturn, the scythe-wielding Roman god of agriculture. Saturnalia was Rome's most anticipated festival, and the god also lent his name to Saturday.

Page 234

PHOTOGRAPHER
H & D Zielske | Getty Images

Bristlecone pine.
California, USA

Bristlecone pine trees, like this one in the Inyo National Forest of California's Eastern Sierra, are believed to live longer than any other organism – up to 5000 years.

Page 235

PHOTOGRAPHER
Paul Chesley | Getty Images

Barnard Glacier.
Alaska, USA

This glacier ploughs slowly through the Wrangell–St Elias National Park, where nine of North America's 16 highest peaks lie, dragging trails of moraine.

Page 236

PHOTOGRAPHER
Frans Lanting | Getty Images

Saint-Trojan-les-Bains.
Île d'Oléron, France

Ocean waves are formed by wind, which is generated, ultimately, by the sun. Tides are caused by the gravitational pull of the moon and the sun.

Page 237

PHOTOGRAPHER
Francis Leroy | Getty Images

Bagan temples.
Mandalay, Myanmar

Bagan was the capital of a pre-Myanmar kingdom; it was both a spiritual place, with 2000 temples remaining from 10,000, and a secular place of scholarship.

Page 238

PHOTOGRAPHER
Johnny Haglund | Getty Images

Chamonix.
Rhône-Alpes, France

The cycles of the moon, including eclipses, have been predicted for thousand of years to come. The pattern is dependent on the movements of the sun, the moon and Earth.

Page 240

PHOTOGRAPHER
Max Homand | Getty Images

San Rafael waterfall.
Ecuador

The Coca River cascades 150m to create Ecuador's largest waterfall. It lies in the important ecosystem of the Sumaco Biosphere Reserve, where the Andean and Amazonian regions meet.

Front Cover Jacket
PHOTOGRAPHER
Shobeir Ansar | Getty Images

Rock Islands
Southern Lagoon.
Palau, Micronesia

The 445 uninhabited limestone or coral islets in the western Pacific Ocean were made a Unesco World Heritage Site in 2012 due to their biodiversity and human history.

Back Cover Jacket
PHOTOGRAPHER
Bob Krist | Corbis

The Empty Quarter.
Saudi Arabia

Rub' al Khali, the Empty Quarter, is a 650,000 sq km (and growing) expanse of sand dunes and salt flats close to the border with Oman. In the past, camel caravans would carry frankincense across the desert.

Back Cover Jacket
PHOTOGRAPHER
George Steinmetz | Corbis

Surin Islands Marine
National Park.
Thailand

Richelieu Rock is a horseshoe-shaped reef discovered by Jacques-Yves Cousteau in the Andaman Sea. The coral attracts a wide range of marine life and lots of scuba divers.

Inside Cover Jacket
PHOTOGRAPHER
F. Stuart Westmorland | Corbis

Beech forest.
Germany

Germany's ancient beech forests are a Unesco World Heritage Site. The trees, which grow to 35m in height, are bright green in spring and turn a russet, golden-bronze in autumn.

Inside Cover Jacket
PHOTOGRAPHER
AVTG | istockphoto.com

Flamingos at Lake Bogoria.
Rift Valley, Kenya

Lesser flamingos, up to two million at a time, feed on the blue-green algae that flourishes in the alkaline waters of Lake Bogoria in northern Kenya.

Inside Cover Jacket
PHOTOGRAPHER
Martin Harvey | Getty Images

Rufous hummingbird.
California, USA

Rufous hummingbirds, here seen feeding on nectar at Huntington Beach, California, are just 8cm long but the hyperactive birds migrate across North America, following the blooming of wild flowers.

Page 2
PHOTOGRAPHER
Susan Gary | Getty Images

Wrangell–St Elias
National Park.
Alaska, USA

The advice on entering this park, which is larger than Switzerland and has few marked hiking trails, is to carry maps, extra food and a bear-proof canister.

Page 4
PHOTOGRAPHER
Frans Lanting | Getty Images

White Sands National
Monument.
New Mexico, USA

Sparkling gypsum sand undulates across the Chihuahuan Desert in south-central New Mexico. It formed from the erosion of selenite crystals that were once up to 1m in length.

Page 255
PHOTOGRAPHER
Radius Images | Getty Images

LONELY PLANET'S
BEAUTIFUL
WORLD

PUBLISHED

October 2013

PUBLISHING DIRECTOR

Piers Pickard

PUBLISHER

Ben Handicott

ART DIRECTION

Mark Adams

PROJECT MANAGER

Robin Barton

PRE-PRESS PRODUCTION

Ryan Evans

PRINT PRODUCTION

Larissa Frost

THANKS

Adrian Blackburn, Bridget Blair, Karina Dea,

Chris Girdler, Will Gourlay, Jane Hart, Florian Poppe,

Rebecca Skinner, Gerard Walker

PUBLISHED BY LONELY PLANET PUBLICATIONS PTY LTD

90 Maribyrnong St, Footscray, Victoria 3011, Australia

ABN 36 005 607 983

ISBN 978 1 74321 717 7

PRINTED IN CHINA

10 9 8 7 6 5 4 3 2 1

AUSTRALIA

90 Maribyrnong St, Footscray, Victoria, 3011

PHONE 03 8379 8000 **FAX** 03 8379 8111

USA

150 Linden St, Oakland, CA 94607

PHONE 510 250 6400 **TOLL FREE** 800 275 8555

UNITED KINGDOM

BBC Worldwide, Media Centre, 201 Wood Lane, London, W12 7TQ

PHONE 020 8433 1333 **FAX** 020 8702 0112

MIX
Paper from
responsible sources
FSC™ C021741

Paper in this book is certified against the Forest Stewardship Council™ standards. FSC™ promotes environmentally responsible, socially beneficial and economically viable management of the world's forests.

ISBN 978-1-74321-717-7

53999